This colorful book introduces young children to the idea of time in relation to things that they do, see and experience throughout a day.

For each hour, the pictures illustrate a variety of activities which could be taking place and the simple text asks a question designed to promote discussion about the child's own experiences.

Available in Series S808

* a is for apple
I can count
Tell me the time
Colors and shapes
* Nursery rhymes

*Ladybird Wall Murals *are also available in these subject areas.*

LADYBIRD BOOKS, INC.
Auburn, Maine 04210 U.S.A.
© LADYBIRD BOOKS LTD 1981
Loughborough, Leicestershire, England

Printed in England

Tell me the time

written by LYNNE BRADBURY

illustrated by LYNN N. GRUNDY

Ladybird Books

Tell me the time... it's 7 o'clock

Time to wake up.
Get out of bed
and get washed.
Can you get dressed by yourself?

Tell me the time... it's 8 o'clock

Time for breakfast.
You could have cornflakes or eggs
or toast or fruit.
What do you like to eat for breakfast?

Tell me the time... it's 9 o'clock

Time to wash the dishes.
Dry the spoons; dry the cups.
How many plates?
Do you help wash and dry the dishes?

Tell me the time... it's 10 o'clock

Time to go out and play.
Play with your toys; ride your bike;
run with your friends.
What games do you like to play?

Tell me the time... it's 11 o'clock

Time for a drink.
You could have milk or juice.
Mom and Dad like coffee.
What do you like to drink?

Tell me the time... it's 12 o'clock

Time to help Mom and Dad.
Dad is working indoors.
Mom is washing the car.
Do you like to help at home?

Tell me the time... it's 1 o'clock

Time to have lunch.
Eat it all up; your favorite dessert
might be next.
What do you like to eat?

Tell me the time ... it's 2 o'clock

Time to go shopping.
Buy some food; buy some new shoes.
The bags are very heavy.
Do you like to go shopping?

Tell me the time... it's 3 o'clock

Time to play with your friends.
Play on the swings or
go down the slide.
What do you do in the park?

Tell me the time... it's 4 o'clock

Time for your television program,
or you could look at a book,
or draw a picture.
What do you like to watch on television?

Tell me the time... it's 5 o'clock

Today is special. It's time for a party.
Lots of food and games
with your friends.
Have you been to a party?

Happy
Birthday

Tell me the time ... it's 6 o'clock

Time to get ready for bed.
Get undressed; have a bath.
It's time for a story.
Which is your favorite story?

Tell me the time... it's 7 o'clock

Time to go to sleep.
It's been a very busy day.
Good night. See you tomorrow!